Original title:
When I Stayed

Copyright © 2024 Swan Charm
All rights reserved.

Author: Olivia Oja
ISBN HARDBACK: 978-9916-89-973-1
ISBN PAPERBACK: 978-9916-89-974-8
ISBN EBOOK: 978-9916-89-975-5

A Dance of the Faithful

In quiet prayer, the hearts unite,
With whispered hopes that reach the light.
A sacred bond, forever strong,
In harmony, we find our song.

Each step a pledge, each turn a vow,
To walk in grace, to humbly bow.
With every rhythm, spirits soar,
In faith, our souls, they will restore.

Through trials faced, through joys we share,
Together we rise, a fervent prayer.
In every dance, His love we greet,
A journey long, yet bittersweet.

With hands held high, we seek the way,
In dreams of peace, we wish to stay.
The light above, our guiding star,
In every step, He is not far.

So let us dance, with hearts ablaze,
In unity, we sing His praise.
With faith as fuel, we'll never cease,
In every heartbeat, there's His peace.

Where Faith Finds Its Roots

In silence deep, our spirits soar,
A whisper soft, forevermore.
Each prayer a seed, in fertile ground,
In God's embrace, our strength is found.

With every storm, our anchor stays,
In trials faced, we learn to praise.
Roots intertwined, our hearts aligned,
Through love divine, true peace we find.

Lessons from the Unhurried Heart

In stillness lies the truth we seek,
The gentle breath, the quiet speak.
Patience teaches, with open hands,
In simple joys, God's lighthouses stand.

Time flows slow, as rivers wide,
In nature's arms, we abide.
Moments cherished, like sacred art,
To know His love, we must first start.

In Reverence of Time

Time, a gift, both fragile and grand,
In every tick, we understand.
Seasons change, yet faith remains,
A tapestry of joyous gains.

In ancient tales and whispered lore,
We find the keys to heaven's door.
With every heartbeat, we are blessed,
In God's design, our souls find rest.

Beneath the Canopy of Hope

Beneath the sky, so vast and bright,
We gather strength, emboldened light.
The stars above, like prayers ascend,
In hope we trust, our truest friend.

Each leaf that rustles tells a tale,
Of faith unbroken, love that won't fail.
Together here, we lift our gaze,
In gratitude, our hearts ablaze.

Trusting the Divine Pause

In silence deep, we find our peace,
The heart inclines, and worries cease.
Through whispered winds, His voice we hear,
In every pause, God draws us near.

Each moment still, a sacred breath,
Transcending fear, defying death.
In every doubt, His light shines bright,
A guiding star in darkest night.

With faith as strong as mountains high,
We trust His ways, though we can't fly.
In hands of grace, our souls will rest,
For in His love, we are truly blessed.

Moments of Contemplation

Beneath the sky, our thoughts take wing,
In quietude, we hear Him sing.
The murmurs soft, of ancient lore,
In stillness, we discover more.

A gentle breeze, like thoughts divine,
Reflects His path, a sacred line.
The world retreats, our spirits soar,
In contemplation, we seek the core.

With every breath, we pause to see,
The hand of God in mystery.
In every sigh, the heart's intent,
Moments of grace, our souls as rent.

The Benevolent Haven

In fields of hope, we find a place,
A haven wrapped in boundless grace.
With arms of love, He shelters all,
In tender whispers, we hear His call.

Through trials faced, we seek the calm,
In every storm, His soothing balm.
Each step we take, His light will guide,
In sacred trust, we won't divide.

A refuge found in hearts united,
In every tear, His love ignited.
The world may wane, but we will stand,
Together, safe in His guiding hand.

Foundations of Belief

With roots that sink into the Earth,
Our faith is built, our sacred birth.
In every trial, we forge our way,
A sturdy path where light will stay.

The teachings old, like rivers flow,
In timeless truths, our spirits glow.
Through trials faced, we rise again,
In unity, we share the pain.

With every word, His love we spread,
A house of faith where none will dread.
In joy and sorrow, we find our place,
Foundations strong in His embrace.

The Whispering Soul

In the silence of the night,
The heart begins to yearn,
For whispers from above,
In gentle breezes, learn.

A voice, soft as a sigh,
Calls forth from shadows deep,
With every breath, reply,
In faith, our spirits leap.

The stars, they dance and gleam,
As messages unfold,
Within the quiet dream,
The love of God behold.

Each moment, grace bestows,
In stillness, truth is found,
With open hands, we close,
Our fears, in peace unbound.

Embrace the sacred light,
Let shadows fade away,
In whispers, find the might,
To trust and softly pray.

A Pilgrim's Rest

Upon the winding path,
A weary heart finds peace,
In every step, a math,
Of grace and sweet release.

The stones may bruise the feet,
Yet wisdom's tender glow,
In trials, love we meet,
As seedlings strive to grow.

Beneath the ancient trees,
Where whispers hush the fright,
A sacred breeze shall tease,
Our souls to take to flight.

In quietude we find,
The strength to carry on,
With faith, our hearts entwined,
A bond that can't be drawn.

As twilight softly falls,
We gather 'round the fire,
And in the stillness calls,
The warmth of our desire.

In the Thicket of Prayer

In the thicket of prayer,
Where whispers intertwine,
The soul an open fare,
To grace, our hearts align.

Branches stretch above,
With leaves that gently sway,
In every word and love,
A truth that lights the way.

Nestled in this space,
Where silence finds its song,
We seek the holy grace,
To guide us, brave and strong.

Each moment still, we breathe,
In faith, our burdens shed,
Within, a light we weave,
With every tear we tread.

In sacred hours spent here,
Our spirits take their flight,
Through winding paths so clear,
To love, the purest light.

The Footprints of Wisdom

Along the sandy shore,
Where tides and memories meet,
Footprints tell the lore,
Of journeys bittersweet.

In every mark engraved,
A story waits in time,
With lessons lightly paved,
In rhythm and in rhyme.

The echoes of the wise,
Resonate through the air,
Like stars that light the skies,
Their brilliance, bright and rare.

Upon the road we tread,
With faith as our compass,
Through trials, never dread,
In love, we find our trust.

So heed the wisdom's call,
In shadows, let us grow,
For footprints mark us all,
In grace, our spirits glow.

In the Light of His Love

In stillness of prayer, we seek His grace,
Each whisper of hope, a warm embrace.
Through shadows we walk, hand in hand,
Guided by faith, in this sacred land.

His light shines bright, dispelling the night,
With each tender moment, our hearts take flight.
In trials we find, our spirit renewed,
For in His love, we are ever imbued.

We gather as one, a family of dreams,
Through valleys of doubt, His guide ever beams.
With courage we rise, against every tide,
In the light of His love, forever we'll bide.

A Sacred Retreat

In solitude's hush, we find our peace,
A space for our souls, where worries cease.
Nature surrounds us, a blessing divine,
In each rustling leaf, His presence we find.

Here hearts are mended, and spirits restored,
In silence we listen, to our holy accord.
With every sunrise, hope fills the air,
In this sacred retreat, we lay ourselves bare.

As dawn breaks anew, we cherish each breath,
Finding in stillness, the beauty of rest.
With gratitude rising, we share in His grace,
In this sacred retreat, we find our place.

The Unseen Traveler

Along winding paths, His footprints are found,
In every soft sigh, and whispering sound.
Though unseen, He walks, beside us each day,
Lighting our journey, guiding our way.

With open hearts, we embrace the unknown,
In darkness and doubt, He's never alone.
For every tear shed, each joy that is shared,
The unseen traveler, His love has declared.

He beckons us forth, through the trials we face,
In shadows of fear, He offers grace.
Though storms may arise, our spirits will soar,
With faith as our anchor, we'll deepen our lore.

Bound by Belief

In the warmth of His love, our spirits unite,
Bound by belief, we shine ever bright.
Through promises whispered, our hearts interlace,
In the tapestry woven, we find our place.

Though storms may rage, our faith will not wane,
Together in prayer, we'll rise through the pain.
With strength in our hearts, we gather in trust,
In the bond of belief, we'll rise from the dust.

Let love be our guide, in each word that we speak,
With kindness and courage, we strengthen the weak.
In the ties that we share, compassion will thrive,
Bound by belief, our spirit's alive.

The Refuge of Serenity

In the stillness of the dawn,
A whisper of grace draws near,
Where shadows fall and peace is born,
The heart finds solace here.

Beneath the ancient oak's embrace,
I kneel with humble plea,
In every moment, His love I trace,
And set my troubled spirit free.

The brook's soft song, a sacred hymn,
Flows gently through the land,
Where every worry starts to dim,
I rest in His outstretched hand.

Guided by the morning light,
I walk this path of grace,
In the refuge of His might,
I find my rightful place.

With every step, a prayer I weave,
Of hope and trust so deep,
In the refuge where I believe,
My soul has found its keep.

Labyrinth of Faith

In the shadows of the night,
A winding path appears,
Where doubt and hope unite,
My heart releases fears.

Each twist and turn, a lesson learned,
In prayer, I seek the way,
With every step, my spirit burned,
In this sacred, holy play.

Walls of stone may rise around,
Yet love will pierce the veil,
In every echo, a truth is found,
As faith begins to sail.

Through trials faced and burdens borne,
I journey to the light,
From ashes of despair reborn,
I turn my heart to fight.

And though the path feels long and steep,
I trust in grace's art,
Within this maze, my soul shall leap,
For faith will guide my heart.

A Sanctuary of Memories

In a garden of golden days,
I gather petals of the past,
With laughter echoing in soft rays,
Each moment blooms and lasts.

The fragrance of love in the air,
A tapestry woven fine,
In every corner, whispers there,
Of those who walked in line.

Beneath the arch of ancient trees,
I ponder the paths we've roamed,
In every breeze, the sweetest pleas,
In this place, our hearts called home.

The sun sets low on golden fields,
As twilight softly creeps,
In this refuge, the soul reveals,
The memories that it keeps.

Forever cherished, gently held,
Each story finds its part,
In this sanctuary, love compelled,
Awakens every heart.

Mysteries of the Heart

In the silence, secrets dwell,
Whispers of the soul's deep yearn,
In every beat, a tale to tell,
Of love's eternal turn.

Beneath the layers, shadows play,
Truth and longing intertwined,
As night transforms the light of day,
The soul's song, unconfined.

Through trials faced, and joys embraced,
I journey into the unknown,
Each step taken, by grace embraced,
In mysteries, I've grown.

The heart, a vessel of pure light,
Guided by a gentle hand,
In every wrong, I seek the right,
In faith, I learn to stand.

So let the heart's mysteries unfurl,
In love's embrace, I abide,
For in this dance, the spirit swirls,
With every pulse, a guide.

The Sanctified Breath

In silent whispers, hearts connect,
With sacred breath, we seek the light.
Echoed prayers in stillness rise,
Gone are fears, renewed in sight.

The dawn ignites with holy grace,
Each moment holds a thread of hope.
We journey forth, our spirits linked,
In divine love, we learn to cope.

Time dances close, a sacred thread,
In every sigh, a promise grows.
With every heartbeat, truth is fed,
In faith's embrace, our spirit flows.

Through trials faced, we will endure,
With fervent hearts, we rise anew.
In bonds of faith, we find our cure,
The sanctified breath, forever true.

Hearth of the Spirit

Within the glow of sacred space,
Where love ignites the inner flame.
We gather close, in warmth embrace,
Around the hearth, we call His name.

The flickering light, a beacon bright,
In darkest hours, it guides our way.
With every prayer, we claim delight,
In unity, our souls will stay.

As shadows blend, and moments cease,
Our voices rise like fragrant prayers.
In every heart, we seek the peace,
That dwells beyond our earthly cares.

With grateful hearts, we share the song,
Of love that binds, and faith that heals.
In spirit's bond, we all belong,
The hearth of God, where love reveals.

Pilgrimage of the Soul

A journey paved with steps of grace,
Each path reveals a story told.
In every turn, we find our place,
With faith as our guide, we are bold.

The mountains high, the valleys low,
In trust, we walk through day and night.
With every breath, we come to know,
The sacred truth, our guiding light.

The miles we tread, though often long,
Are filled with blessings vast and pure.
In trials met, we grow more strong,
The pilgrimage leads to what's sure.

Through every storm, through every tear,
We gather strength from love divine.
In whispers soft, His voice we hear,
The soul's pilgrimage, forever shine.

Time Enveloped in Prayer

In every moment, stillness found,
The breath of heaven meets our plea.
In sacred time, our hearts are bound,
To grace that flows eternally.

The clock ticks slow, yet time stands still,
In quietude, the world fades away.
Our spirits lift, with fervor and will,
In whispered hopes, we choose to pray.

The tapestry of life we weave,
With threads of faith intertwined.
In each petition, we believe,
The divine plan has been designed.

The hours pass, as blessings flow,
In prayerful hearts, we find our peace.
In time enveloped, love will grow,
And in His light, our doubts shall cease.

The Path of Inner Light

In stillness, whispers rise,
Guiding souls through darkened skies.
A flicker shines, a beacon bright,
Illuminating the inner sight.

Faith's embrace, a gentle hand,
Leading hearts on sacred land.
With every step, a chance to grow,
In the light, true wisdom flows.

The road is long, yet never alone,
In unity, love is sown.
Through trials faced, and shadows cast,
The light within shall hold steadfast.

Each moment cherished, sacred space,
An open heart finds its grace.
As stars align and spirits soar,
The path unfolds forevermore.

Gathering Sacred Moments

In quietude, we find our way,
Gathering moments of each day.
Like droplets fall from heaven's grace,
Each second holds a sacred place.

In laughter shared and love's embrace,
We weave the threads of time and space.
The breath of life, a hymn we sing,
Awakens joy in everything.

Through open eyes, the world unfolds,
In simple acts, the heart beholds.
As seasons change, so do our dreams,
In gathering light, the spirit gleams.

Let us pause, reflect, and see,
The beauty in our unity.
For every moment, a treasure sought,
In sacred space, our souls are taught.

Heartstrings of Hope

In shadows deep, hope softly calls,
Echoing through these sacred halls.
With tender strings, the heart will play,
A melody that lights the way.

With each heartbeat, resilience grows,
In valleys low, the spirit knows.
Together we rise, despite the strife,
In unity, we find new life.

The dawn shall break, the sun will rise,
Painting colors in the skies.
With every breath, we shall believe,
In heartstrings woven, we achieve.

So let us sing, a song of grace,
In trials faced, we find our place.
For hope remains, a guiding light,
In every soul, it shines so bright.

Searching for Solace

In the stillness of the morn,
A gentle whisper, a heart reborn.
Through sorrow's veil, we seek to find,
The peace that soothes the restless mind.

In nature's arms, we lay our cares,
Finding solace in whispered prayers.
The rustling leaves, a soft refrain,
Echoing through our joy and pain.

With every breath, we start anew,
In the heart of silence, love shines through.
Amidst the storms, a calm aligns,
In searching souls, true strength entwines.

May we embrace the sacred quest,
To find the calm, the heart's true rest.
In gracious moments, solace found,
Each sacred breath, forever bound.

The Sacred Interlude

In a quiet grove, the spirit speaks,
Whispers of truth in soft, gentle peaks.
Nature's embrace, a divine retreat,
Where hearts align, and souls find their beat.

Amidst the stillness, a prayer takes flight,
Guided by stars that adorn the night.
Each leaf a hymn, each breeze a sigh,
Woven together, our voices rise high.

Reflections shimmer on the water's face,
Offering solace, a sacred space.
In the hush of dawn, the world anew,
Awakens the heart to wonder, to view.

From depths of silence, wisdom appears,
Softening burdens, allaying our fears.
In sacred moments, we find our grace,
A connection woven, time can't erase.

So let us gather, in love and light,
Treading softly, our spirits in flight.
In the sacred interlude, we come to know,
The beauty of faith, in the stillness, we grow.

In Silent Reverence

In silent reverence, we bow our heads,
Acknowledging the path that gently spreads.
With every heartbeat, a prayer is sung,
Echoes of gratitude forever sprung.

The sacred whispers weave through the trees,
Carrying dreams on a tender breeze.
With open hearts, we seek the divine,
In the stillness, our spirits align.

A tapestry rich with the threads of grace,
Every moment, a sacred embrace.
In nature's cathedral, we humbly dwell,
Life's whispered secrets, a story to tell.

Beneath the heavens, we find our peace,
In silent moments, our worries cease.
Through shadows of doubt, the light will guide,
In silent reverence, with love as our tide.

So let us listen, to whispers unfold,
In the quiet of hearts, and the stories retold.
In the stillness, we'll gather as one,
A chorus of souls beneath the sun.

Tapestry of Still Moments

In the loom of time, still moments weave,
Threads of quietude, we gently receive.
Peace spills over like water from springs,
A tapestry vibrant, where presence clings.

Beneath the arching skies, we find our way,
Each breath a blessing, guiding the day.
With open arms, we embrace the calm,
In stillness, we dwell, inhaling the balm.

The minutiae of life, a sacred art,
Every fleeting second, a chance to impart.
In the whispers of nature, the heart hears true,
A tapestry woven, in colors anew.

Moments collected like pearls on a strand,
Each one a treasure, lovingly planned.
In the quiet unfolding, we find our space,
Nestled in solace, surrounded by grace.

So let us cherish the stillness we find,
In the tapestry, our hearts intertwined.
Moments that shimmer, like stars up above,
In the sacred stillness, we tap into love.

The Hushed Pilgrimage

On the path of life, we take each step,
In hushed pilgrimage, where silence is kept.
With candlelight flickers, our souls ignite,
Guided by faith through the endless night.

As we wander, the heart's compass leads,
In stillness, we sow the kindest of seeds.
Nature unfolds, with every soft breath,
A sacred journey, where love conquers death.

Mountains stand tall, their wisdom profound,
Each rustling leaf sings a heavenly sound.
In the arms of creation, we find our way,
Through the valleys of shadow, to light's bright array.

Footfalls in harmony, the silence abounds,
With echoes of peace, in soft, sacred rounds.
In this hushed pilgrimage, we seek to know,
The grace that ignites and divinely flows.

So let us tread lightly, with hearts open wide,
In the hush of our journey, with love as our guide.
Together we walk, in this sacred trance,
In the hush of existence, we dance our dance.

The Turning Leaves of Prayer

In whispers soft, the leaves do turn,
Each whisper holds a sacred yearn.
The branches sway in gentle grace,
Divine embrace in nature's space.

A moment still, the heart takes flight,
In every prayer, a spark of light.
Like autumn hues, we seek to find,
The love that binds all humankind.

With every breath, a leaf falls down,
A tribute to the holy crown.
In rustling tones, we hear the voice,
In turning leaves, our hearts rejoice.

Beneath the sky, the silence calls,
In nature's arms, our spirit sprawls.
The turning leaves, a symphony,
Of prayerful hearts in unity.

So let us walk among the trees,
And dance with grace upon the breeze.
In turning leaves, our souls awake,
The prayers we share, the paths we take.

The Stillness Between Verses

In stillness deep, where shadows meet,
The sacred pause, a heartbeat sweet.
Between the words, the silence glows,
In quietude, our spirit knows.

Each verse a step, each breath a prayer,
In tranquil spaces, love laid bare.
The echoes linger, softly play,
In hush of night, they drift away.

The stars above reflect our quest,
In stillness rich, our souls find rest.
We weave the threads of night and day,
In sacred pause, we learn to pray.

The silence sings of hope and grace,
In quiet moments, we embrace.
The stillness births a holy song,
In every heart, where we belong.

So let us linger in the calm,
With open hands, a gentle balm.
In stillness pure, our spirits soar,
The space between, forevermore.

In Sacred Silence

In sacred silence, whispers rise,
The hidden truths beneath the skies.
The quiet voice that guides the soul,
In stillness we become made whole.

The rhythm of the heart beats slow,
In every pause, the spirit flows.
In sacred space, the light reveals,
The depth of love that gently heals.

With every breath, we find the way,
In quiet moments, we shall stay.
The silence wraps like warm embrace,
Reflecting light upon our face.

In shadows deep, the holy spark,
Ignites the flame within the dark.
In sacred silence, we unite,
The whispered prayer, our hearts ignite.

So let us dwell in peace profound,
In sacred silence, love is found.
With open hearts, we softly tread,
In every silence, truth is fed.

Echoes of Devotion

In echoes sweet, devotion sings,
A melody of gentle wings.
With every prayer, a ripple flows,
In heartfelt sighs, the spirit glows.

The chant of love, a sacred thread,
In every note, the soul is fed.
With every heartbeat, our voices rise,
In echoes of joy, the heavens sigh.

To all who seek in darkest night,
The echoes guide like stars so bright.
In every tone, a truth laid bare,
The whispers dance in holy air.

Through mountains high and valleys low,
In echoes strong, our faith shall grow.
The path of light, our spirits find,
In echoes of love, we are intertwined.

So let us sing, united we stand,
In echoes of devotion, hand in hand.
With fervent hearts, we pave the way,
In every echo, our prayers stay.

Reflections in the Holy Veil

In shadows cast by sacred light,
I seek the truth, a softer sight.
Each whisper speaks of grace we find,
Within the veil, all hearts aligned.

In the stillness, prayers take flight,
Bathed in love, dispelling night.
The soul ascends on wings of praise,
In the presence, I long to stay.

With every tear, a flower blooms,
In sacred spaces, hope consumes.
Reflections dance, a holy fray,
In unity, we find our way.

Guided by the stars above,
Embraced by gentle hands of love.
The heart's desire, a guiding star,
In holy silence, we wander far.

In moments pure, I glimpse the grace,
Within the veil, a holy place.
The tapestry of faith unfolds,
In whispers soft, the truth beholds.

The Slow Dance of Reverence

In twilight's glow, our spirits meet,
A rhythm soft, in quiet seat.
The heartbeat of the ancient song,
We sway together, right and wrong.

Each step is filled with holy care,
Where angels tread, we rest our share.
With humble hearts, we join the dance,
In grace and mercy, find our chance.

The winding path of faith revealed,
In every heart, a promise sealed.
A journey long, yet filled with light,
In sacred moves, we take our flight.

With every turn, the spirit glows,
In the embrace, compassion flows.
With reverence deep, and purpose clear,
We dance through doubt, we conquer fear.

In love's expanse, our souls entwine,
In this holy dance, we shall shine.
The slow dance shares our living truth,
In every step, reclaim our youth.

A Covenant of Being

In sacred vows, we bind our hearts,
In quiet faith, our journey starts.
A promise made, through trials and tears,
A tapestry woven throughout the years.

With each sunrise, our spirits rise,
In the embrace of endless skies.
We walk together, hand in hand,
In this covenant, we firmly stand.

The sacred breath of life we share,
Awakens hope, a constant prayer.
In every moment, love takes flight,
In gentle whispers, guiding light.

Through storms that rage and winds that howl,
The bond we share does not disavow.
In faith's embrace, we find our peace,
A sacred union that will not cease.

In twilight's glow, we raise our voice,
Our covenant, our joyous choice.
With every heartbeat, we renew,
A promise sealed, forever true.

Inward Journey of the Faithful

Within the heart, a pathway lies,
To sacred spaces, we silently rise.
In meditative silence, I explore,
The depths of spirit, forevermore.

With every breath, the stillness grows,
In gentle waves, the spirit flows.
The inward journey, a sacred quest,
In discovery, our souls find rest.

When shadows call, I turn within,
Unraveling threads of loss and sin.
With open arms, I greet the night,
In darkness, I find hidden light.

Through valleys deep and mountains tall,
The faithful rise, responding to the call.
In solitude, connections bloom,
Illuminating every room.

With each step taken, wisdom grows,
In grace's arms, the spirit knows.
The inward journey leads us home,
In every heart, we shall not roam.

Timeless Pursuits of the Soul

In silence, truth begins to rise,
The heart seeks light, beneath the skies.
Each prayer a whisper, soft and clear,
A journey inward, drawing near.

With open hands, we seek the grace,
In every moment, find our place.
The sacred dance of love unfolds,
A tapestry of faith retold.

In shadows, hope ignites the flame,
A force within that calls our name.
Through trials faced, the soul does grow,
As rivers of mercy freely flow.

For every heart, a distinct song,
A melody where we belong.
In timeless quests, we find our aim,
A legacy, yet not the same.

With every step, the path reveals,
The truth that breathes, the spirit heals.
Within the stillness, wisdom sighs,
A beacon bright in endless skies.

Illuminated Paths of Patience

In gentle whispers, time unfolds,
The waiting heart, in silence holds.
With every breath, a chance to see,
The deeper truths that set us free.

Like autumn leaves on winding trails,
The soul's sweet journey never fails.
Patience, a jewel, so rare and bright,
Guides through the shadows, towards the light.

In quiet moments, faith ignites,
As dawn approaches, filling nights.
Each heartbeat echoes love's embrace,
A promise held in sacred space.

Through storms that rage and skies that weep,
The soul finds strength in valleys deep.
For every trial, a lesson learned,
In every pause, the heart discerned.

As stars illuminate the dark,
The gentle flicker, a holy spark.
In pathways rich with sacred grace,
We walk with patience, in His embrace.

In the Calm of the Spirit

When chaos swirls, the spirit steadies,
A tranquil heart, against the eddies.
Within the storm, a stillness grows,
The peace of heaven softly flows.

In morning light, calm spirits rise,
A chorus sung to endless skies.
Each moment spent in holy rest,
Reveals the truth; the soul's lifelong quest.

Let breaths become a prayerful song,
Where each note finds where we belong.
In sacred quiet, wisdom blooms,
As laughter dances through the rooms.

In every heartbeat, grace abounds,
A symphony of holy sounds.
In the calm, we feel His sway,
Guiding our steps, come what may.

With gentle whispers, love's embrace,
In every trial, see His face.
For in the still, the spirit glows,
A beacon bright, as pure life flows.

The Sanctuary of Seeking

In the sacred woods, I wander slow,
Each step reveals what hearts can know.
With every rustle, a voice so clear,
The language of mercy, drawing near.

The dawn brings hopes, like petals wide,
In the sanctuary, truth will bide.
With open eyes, we seek the way,
In every shadow, light will play.

A timeless quest, we dare to find,
In the heart of silence, love unbind.
As rivers flow and mountains rise,
The soul is led by sacred ties.

Through every gate that we must face,
The sanctuary holds its grace.
Within these walls, the spirit sings,
The joy of life that seeking brings.

In gentle whispers, guidance flows,
A heavenly path, where faith bestows.
In our searching, hearts align,
For every step, the stars will shine.

Veils of Solitude

In the stillness, whispers flow,
Veils of solitude gently grow.
A sacred space, a quiet plea,
Hearts entwined in mystery.

Each shadow holds a prayer within,
Guiding souls, where light begins.
In the depths of night's embrace,
Finding truth in unseen grace.

Waves of silence softly rise,
Cradled in the starry skies.
Lonely paths lead us to find,
The answers buried in the mind.

Beneath the stars, the spirit sings,
Unlocking all the hidden things.
Veils unfold in sacred light,
Bearing gifts from realms of night.

In the silence, wisdom stands,
A gentle touch of divine hands.
With every breath, we seek the one,
In solitude, our journey's begun.

Sanctum of Silence

In the sanctum, peace resides,
Where the raging tempest hides.
Quiet whispers turn to prayer,
In the love that fills the air.

Hearts unite in soft refrain,
Beneath the weight of earthly pain.
Stillness wraps us in its cloak,
As hope rekindles with each stroke.

Voices echo in the void,
Between the breaths, all fears destroyed.
A hallowed ground of sacred space,
Here we find our rightful place.

The silence teaches, deep and wise,
Unveiling truths that never die.
In solitude, we find the light,
Guiding us from dark to bright.

Longing souls find solace near,
In the hushed, we conquer fear.
The sanctum holds a gentle grace,
Where divinity we can trace.

Echoes of the Divine

In the still, the echoes call,
Reverberating through us all.
A melody of love profound,
In every heartbeat, it is found.

Voices rising, soft and clear,
Whispers meant for all who hear.
Threads of grace intertwine and weave,
In each moment, we believe.

Rays of light pierce through the haze,
Guiding lost souls through the maze.
Each echo tells a sacred tale,
In the spirit, we shall prevail.

Harmonies of pure delight,
Illuminating darkest night.
With each echo, silent prayer,
We feel the touch of love laid bare.

In the distance, a voice calls home,
Through every heart, we start to roam.
Echoes of the divine inspire,
Fueling souls with sacred fire.

In the Embrace of the Everlasting

In the embrace of timeless truth,
We find the echoes of our youth.
Moments linger, sweet and bold,
Stories of the heart retold.

Hands entwined in sacred trust,
Whispers lit by stardust.
Every sigh and breath we take,
In this love, our spirits wake.

Beneath the canopy of night,
Finding solace in the light.
Eternal warmth, a guiding hand,
Bringing peace to this vast land.

As time unfolds, we walk the way,
In the presence, come what may.
Every heartbeat echoes deep,
In the embrace, our souls shall keep.

With every dawn, the cycle spins,
A timeless dance where love begins.
In the everlasting, we find grace,
Embraced within this sacred space.

Foundations of the Unseen

In silence deep, His wisdom calls,
A whisper heard through ancient walls.
The faith we build on unseen ground,
In every heart, His truth is found.

From shadows cast, His light breaks free,
A promise held in mystery.
With every prayer, we seek the way,
To walk with Him, our fears at bay.

The path may wind, the journey long,
Yet in His grace, we find our song.
Trusting not in what we see,
But clinging fast to faith's decree.

Each step we take, with hearts aligned,
In divine love, our souls entwined.
The unseen hands that guide our course,
Reveal to us His endless source.

In quietude, our spirits soar,
Foundations strong forevermore.
For in the unseen lies our might,
The faith that anchors us in light.

The Covenant of Rest

In evening's glow, His promise shines,
A covenant of love divine.
In stillness found, our burdens cease,
He offers weary souls their peace.

The weary heart, He bids to stay,
In sacred moments, night and day.
With open arms, He draws us near,
Assuring us that He is here.

Rest in His presence, sweet embrace,
In every trial, His arms we grace.
With gentle whispers, calm our fears,
Through every joy, and all our tears.

The world can wait, His love persists,
In quiet hours, we find the bliss.
A sacred vow, forever blessed,
In every sigh, the covenant of rest.

In trusting Him, we find our home,
With hearts unburdened, freely roam.
The peace we seek, forever lasts,
In His embrace, the shadows cast.

As He Dwells with Me

In sacred space, He walks with me,
A gentle guide, eternally.
Through darkest nights and brightest days,
His presence found in countless ways.

With every breath, I sense His grace,
In whispered prayers, we find our place.
As He dwells close within my soul,
I find my strength, He makes me whole.

In joy and sorrow, hand in hand,
Together we shall ever stand.
The love He gives, a sacred balm,
A harbor safe, a refuge calm.

With every word, I speak His name,
In all my trials, He feels the same.
As darkness falls, His light will shine,
In every moment, He is mine.

As He dwells with me, my heart shall sing,
To Him I lift my offering.
In every breath, I find my plea,
Forever close, as He dwells with me.

Respite in His Light

In morning's grace, His radiance glows,
A refuge sweet, where kindness flows.
In shadow's depths, His warmth is near,
A gentle touch that calms all fear.

With every dawn, my spirit wakes,
In light divine, my heart it takes.
The burdens fade with His embrace,
Respite found in His holy place.

In trials fierce, when hope seems lost,
I trust in Him, whatever the cost.
For every shadow casts a light,
In Him I stand, through darkest night.

His promises are bright and true,
With every beam, He makes all new.
In joyful songs, my soul will rise,
To greet the day, to touch the skies.

Forever blessed, I seek His face,
In every turn, I find my grace.
Respite in His light, my heart's delight,
In faith I stand, through day and night.

Breathing in Sacred Spaces

In quiet halls where echoes dwell,
The heart finds peace, the soul's soft bell.
With every breath, the spirit sings,
In sacred spaces, love transcends all things.

Whispers dance in the light so pure,
Each moment here feels deep and sure.
Hands raised high in grateful prayer,
In this stillness, we find Him there.

The walls enfold our silent trust,
In every heartbeat, faith adjusts.
A sacred bond through time and grace,
In breathing deep, we find our place.

The fragrance of devotion flows,
A gentle breeze, where mercy grows.
As joy unfurls in holy bliss,
In every pause, we find His kiss.

With open hearts and lifted eyes,
We journey forth beneath the skies.
In every breath, a promise made,
In sacred spaces, never to fade.

In the Shadows of Devotion

In the shadows, faith takes flight,
Whispers shared in the fading light.
Hearts entwined in silent prayer,
In devotion's arms, we lay bare.

Beneath the stars, our secrets rise,
Each murmured plea, a soft disguise.
The world fades out, our spirits soar,
In the darkness, we seek Him more.

The gentle warmth of His embrace,
Illuminates each hidden space.
In every tear, a glimmer shows,
In shadows deep, His love still glows.

With whispered hopes, we tread the night,
In the silence, we find His light.
Through moonlit paths, we walk as one,
In the shadows, our journey's begun.

Each sigh ascends, a prayer to keep,
In the stillness, our dreams run deep.
In shadows' grip, we find the way,
To hearts ignited, come what may.

Beneath the Eternal Gaze

Beneath the gaze of heavens wide,
Our souls lay bare, in love we bide.
The stars align, a cosmic plan,
In whispered prayers, we understand.

Each moment lived, a sacred chance,
To join the universe in dance.
With every heartbeat, grace we seek,
In truth, we find the words to speak.

The dawn breaks forth, a canvas bright,
Painting love with shades of light.
In every sunrise, hope reborn,
Beneath His gaze, our hearts are worn.

Vows of love inked in the skies,
Promises sown where the spirit lies.
Through trials faced, we grow in faith,
In every step, His light we chase.

With every breath, we draw Him near,
In sacred quiet, we conquer fear.
Beneath the gaze that sees us whole,
We find the rhythm of our soul.

Threads of Reflection

In threads of thought, we weave our dreams,
With every glance, a story gleams.
Reflections dance on rippling streams,
In silence found, we hear His themes.

Each moment sculpted, time refined,
In gentle whispers, truth aligned.
Through trials faced and joys embraced,
In threads of light, His hope is laced.

With open hearts, we gather near,
In shared reflections, faith appears.
Every tear, a strand so bright,
In weaving love, we find our light.

The loom of life spins tales, refined,
In acts of kindness, love is intertwined.
Embraced by grace, we rise above,
In threads of reflection, we find His love.

Through pain and joy, the tapestry grows,
In every heartbeat, His mercy flows.
Within these threads, our spirit sings,
In harmony, we embrace all things.

The Quietude of Faith

In stillness, hearts do find,
A sanctuary, pure and kind.
Where doubts take flight like birds in air,
Faith blooms gently, a whispered prayer.

In shadows cast by fears so deep,
The light of trust begins to seep.
With every breath, a promise near,
A quietude, dissolving fear.

Each moment held, a sacred thread,
We follow where the Spirit led.
Through storms that rage and trials vast,
Our faith remains, a tether vast.

From valleys low to mountains high,
In every tear, we learn to cry.
With open hearts, we seek the way,
In quietude, we find our sway.

So let us walk, unchained, unbound,
In faith's embrace, our peace is found.
Each step a dance, divine and free,
In quietude, we cease to flee.

A Moment in His Presence

In moments still, His grace descends,
A whisper soft, the heart transcends.
In silence deep, our souls ignite,
A glimpse of love, so pure, so bright.

Beneath the stars, a sacred night,
We bow our heads, we seek His light.
With open arms, His warmth we crave,
In fleeting time, the world, we waive.

Each breath inhaled, a thought divine,
In His embrace, our spirits twine.
Between the beats, joy's echoes sound,
In every heartbeat, love is found.

Let burdens lift, let worries fade,
In His presence, we are remade.
With faith restored, our hope ignites,
In holy pause, our heart unites.

So take a moment, breathe Him near,
In tender space, dissolve all fear.
A moment spent, forever stays,
In love's reflection, we find praise.

Whispers of the Divine

In gentle winds, His whispers call,
A still, small voice that guides us all.
Through rustling leaves and twilight's sigh,
We sense the breath of God nearby.

In every shadow, light revealed,
The mysteries of love unsealed.
With faith as map, we journey forth,
To seek the gem of our true worth.

With every tear, a lesson learned,
In trials faced, our hearts have turned.
For in the struggle, hope takes flight,
As whispers weave through darkest night.

The quiet spaces, lessons keen,
In sacred silence, God is seen.
Through every heartbeat, every breath,
Divine embraces conquer death.

So listen close, His voice is near,
In every joy, in every fear.
The whispers of the Divine unfold,
A tapestry of love retold.

The Grace of Staying

In every season, grace abounds,
In trials faced, true strength is found.
To linger long, to seek, to know,
In moments still, His love will grow.

The path may wander, winds may change,
Yet in His arms, we rearrange.
With faith as anchor, hope our guide,
In grace of staying, we abide.

Each choice embraced, with purpose clear,
In daily steps, He draws us near.
With hearts unleashed, we sense His call,
In gentle strength, we rise, not fall.

So here we stand, come what may,
In every dawn, we find our way.
Each moment cherished, love displayed,
In grace of staying, unafraid.

Let roots grow deep, let branches spread,
In fertile ground, our spirits fed.
With patience woven through each day,
In grace of staying, we shall stay.

The Altar of Everyday Life

On humble hills our spirits rise,
In toil and care, the heart complies.
Each moment sacred, blessed through strife,
We gather strength, the altar of life.

The dawn arrives, a whispered prayer,
In each breath drawn, love's tender care.
In laughter's light, or sorrow's sigh,
We find the grace that won't pass by.

Each meal we share, a holy rite,
In mundane tasks, God shines so bright.
Our hands are clay, our hearts the flame,
In the simple joys, we know His name.

The friends we cherish, the bonds we weave,
In every giving, we do believe.
Through challenges faced, we stand as one,
In the everyday, His will is done.

So let us live, with hearts aligned,
In every moment, His love defined.
The altar waits, it's here we stand,
In the flow of life, we find His hand.

In the Wait of a Promise

Upon the breeze hearts whisper low,
In patient hope, our spirits grow.
Each moment waiting, a lesson learned,
In silent trust, our souls are turned.

The dawn may break with heavy clouds,
Yet faith persists, though fate enshrouds.
Each tear we shed, a seed to sow,
In darkness deep, new light will grow.

We gather strength from days gone by,
A richer tale, we let it lie.
For in the wait, we're shaped and made,
In steadfast love, our fears allayed.

The promise glimmers, a distant star,
In every heart, it's never far.
With each prayer whispered, the dawn will break,
For hope endures, and never shakes.

So hold on tight, dear weary soul,
In every pause, we find the whole.
The promise waits in timeless grace,
In the wait of life, we find His face.

When Stillness Speaks

In quiet moments, the world retreats,
Where heartbeats echo, and spirit greets.
Amidst the chaos, a gentle plea,
When stillness speaks, we're truly free.

The rustle of leaves, a whispered tune,
In nature's arms, we find our boon.
Each moment still, a breath divine,
In silent prayer, His love we find.

The stars above in shimmering grace,
In the night's calm, we seek His face.
In the hush of dusk, the soul ignites,
When stillness speaks, our hearts take flight.

In stillness deep, the wounds are healed,
In quiet trust, our fate revealed.
Each thought released, each fear let go,
In tranquil peace, His wonders flow.

So let us linger where time stands still,
Embrace the calm, the heart to fill.
In every pause, the truth we seek,
When stillness speaks, the spirit's meek.

The Heart's Hidden Sanctuary

In solace found, our spirits bloom,
Within the heart, a quiet room.
Where whispers echo, love resides,
The heart's sanctuary, where peace abides.

Through trials faced, and burdens bare,
In sacred stillness, we lift our prayer.
Each quiet thought, a gentle spark,
In shadows cast, He lights the dark.

With eyes of faith, we seek the truth,
In every storm, we claim our youth.
For in the silence, burdens break,
The heart's retreat, a place to wake.

Beyond the chaos, beyond the noise,
The heart's soft whisper sings of joys.
In every tear, a journey starts,
In hidden sanctuary, we find our hearts.

So let us seek in quiet grace,
The cherished spot, our sacred place.
In love's embrace, the soul's delight,
The heart's hidden sanctuary shines bright.

A Dialogue with the Divine

In silence we meet, the spirit unfolds,
Whispers of love in the stillness behold.
Questions arise from our hearts' weary flight,
In the glow of His wisdom, we find our light.

Each prayer a petal, soft in its grace,
A tapestry woven, in time and in place.
God listens closely, His heart feels our dreams,
In the canvas of faith, hope brightly gleams.

Voices entwined in the sacred exchange,
In the heart of the night, life's path feels strange.
Yet courage is born through the darkest of fears,
In His presence we shed all our burdens and tears.

The world fades away, as we linger near,
Wrapped in the warmth, of the love we hold dear.
In this dialogue sweet, our souls intertwine,
As we walk hand in hand, through the sacred divine.

A Haven of Grace

In a meadow of faith, I find my retreat,
Where grace flows like rivers, and hearts feel complete.
Under the shelter of the old willow tree,
I breathe in His presence, just Him and me.

The whispers of angels caress my weary soul,
In this haven of peace, I've finally found whole.
Each moment a blessing, pure love in the breeze,
In the arms of His mercy, my spirit finds ease.

With every soft sigh, the world falls away,
As I revel in stillness, through night and through day.
Here worries are lifted, in gentle embrace,
I am forever grateful for this haven of grace.

The stars sing a lullaby, lit from above,
In the quiet of night, I'm surrounded by love.
Each heartbeat a prayer, each breath a sweet song,
In this sacred space, I finally belong.

The Stillness of Prayer

In the hush of the morning, I kneel by my side,
With hands gently clasped, in Him I abide.
Each word a soft echo, floating on air,
In the stillness I feel Him, present in prayer.

Time drifts like the clouds, unhurried and slow,
In the whispers of faith, my spirit will grow.
Each moment a treasure, each silence a gift,
In the dance of the heart, my worries do lift.

With eyes turned to Heaven, and heart open wide,
I'm wrapped in His love, like the warmest tide.
In the stillness I find, an unwavering peace,
From the burdens of life, my heart finds release.

The echoes of prayer linger sweet in the air,
With each solemn breath, I feel Him so near.
In stillness I gather the strength to be bold,
In the sanctuary of prayer, my spirit unfolds.

The Heart's Quiet Journey

Upon the winding road, my heart takes its flight,
In search of the truths hidden by night.
Each step a reflection, each whisper a sign,
As the compass of faith gently leads me to find.

In valleys of shadow, the light breaks anew,
With laughter and sorrow, all intertwined too.
The journey unfolds in the softest of ways,
As I nurture my soul through the labor of days.

With eyes set to Heaven and heart open wide,
I wander in wonder, with God as my guide.
In the rhythm of grace, my spirit will soar,
Through hills and through hardships, I'm learning to adore.

Each heartbeat a mantra, a sweet serenade,
In the quiet of moments, where fears start to fade.
The heart's quiet journey, a sacred embrace,
In the light of His love, I find my true place.

Torn Pages of Grace

In the book of life, we write,
Torn pages whisper, shining bright.
Each scar a tale, each tear a prayer,
In grace we find our way to share.

Heaven's light upon our soul,
With faith, we search to feel whole.
Through trials faced, we learn to bend,
In every loss, love's hand will mend.

From shadows deep, we rise anew,
In every breath, a chance to do.
The ink may fade, but hearts remain,
In holy words, we break the chain.

Time may stain the sacred text,
Yet each moment's grace, the next.
With open arms, we welcome strife,
In torn pages, we grasp at life.

So let us turn each page with care,
For grace will find us everywhere.
With faith like wings, we soar above,
In each torn page, we find His love.

In the Stillness I Found

In the stillness of the night,
Whispers soft, a guiding light.
Calm my heart, awaken my mind,
In quiet moments, truth I find.

Stars above like dreams unfold,
Tales of faith and love retold.
In silence deep, His voice will call,
A gentle nudge to heed His thrall.

Time stands still, a sacred space,
Embraced by peace, I seek His grace.
In every breath, His presence near,
A light in darkness, soothing fear.

When the world outside is loud,
And burdens rest like darkened shroud,
I close my eyes, the storm subsides,
In stillness sweet, my spirit glides.

So here I dwell, and here I pray,
In His embrace, I find my way.
With open heart, I lift my sight,
In the stillness, He is my light.

Offering a Heart's Refuge

When weary souls seek solace here,
Offering a heart, pure and clear.
In every prayer, a space to dwell,
Where love and light begin to swell.

Our burdens shared, a load less dense,
With every grace, a holy sense.
In kindness woven, bond grows tight,
Together forging paths of light.

Open hands and hearts aglow,
Amidst the trials, let kindness flow.
Each gentle act, a sacred touch,
A refuge found in giving much.

Let every heartbeat echo true,
With compassion, the world renew.
In this haven, fears take flight,
As faith and hope ignite the night.

So come, my friend, seek shelter here,
In quiet love, cast off your fear.
An offering made, as we embrace,
In hearts united, we find grace.

A Holy Intermission

In life's great play, we take a pause,
A holy intermission, for the cause.
With every act, a brief respite,
In sacred stillness, hearts take flight.

Beneath the stars, we gather round,
In whispered prayers, the lost are found.
With gratitude, we lift our voice,
In every moment, to rejoice.

The world outside may rush and roar,
Yet in this space, we seek and soar.
In shared silence, the spirit speaks,
With love that strengthens, as the heart seeks.

Seasons change, like pages turn,
Yet in this break, we rise and learn.
A truce with time, we gently seek,
In holy peace, the strong and weak.

So let us pause, let worries fade,
In each embrace, the love displayed.
A holy intermission here we find,
In moments soft, hearts intertwined.

The Tapestry of Unrushed Moments

In whispers soft, the morning breaks,
Where time meanders, gently wakes.
Each breath a thread, a sacred weave,
In silence found, the heart believes.

Beneath the arch of heavens wide,
There lies a peace, where dreams abide.
No rush to grasp the fleeting day,
In stillness, find the truest way.

With every dawn, a gift anew,
The sun's embrace, the sky's deep blue.
In harmony, the world unfolds,
A tapestry of warmth retold.

Through every trial, grace will flow,
In moments shared, we come to know.
With patience held in loving hands,
The spirit sings, and joy withstands.

So linger long, in sacred light,
And taste the sweetness, pure and bright.
For in each moment, wild and free,
The heart finds home, eternally.

Hallowed Grounds of Anticipation

Upon the hill where shadows play,
And silence speaks in soft ballet.
The promise stirs within the breeze,
A hope that dances through the trees.

In every sigh, the soul reclaims,
A whispering call, a thousand names.
Each heartbeat echoes through the night,
A beacon glows, a guiding light.

The dawn awakens dreams once sown,
In fertile ground, our faith has grown.
A harvest born from trials faced,
In hallowed ground, our love embraced.

As prayers ascend like smoke to skies,
We greet the morn with reverent eyes.
The past, a scroll of lessons learned,
In every page, our spirits yearned.

So stand with me in this embrace,
As anticipation fills the space.
Together we shall walk this path,
In sacred trust, beyond the wrath.

The Echoing Heartbeat of Faith

In the quiet of the night we pray,
With yearning hearts, we find our way.
Each pulse, a rhythm, strong and true,
The heartbeat calls, and we renew.

Through shadows dark, where doubts may cast,
In whispered creeds, our lot is fast.
A sacred bond that time can't sever,
In faith's embrace, we stand together.

Each tear, a testament to grace,
In trials met, we find our place.
For through the storms, a light will shine,
The echoing heart, forever divine.

With every breath, we seek to find,
The gentle touch of love entwined.
In every struggle, hope's refrain,
The glorious song that breaks our chain.

So let us stand in endless prayer,
With open hearts, our burdens share.
For in this dance of life and breath,
The promise whispered conquers death.

In the Shelter of Solace

In the shadowed glen, we find our peace,
Where troubles fade and worries cease.
In nature's arms, our spirits soar,
A refuge found, forevermore.

The gentle stream, a soothing sound,
In tranquil depths, our savior found.
With every leaf that whispers low,
In solace, love begins to grow.

The stars will guide our wandering eyes,
In night's embrace, our spirits rise.
A sacred bond, unbroken, whole,
In stillness, whispers soothe the soul.

The dawn will break and joy will bloom,
As sunlight chases away the gloom.
In every moment spent in grace,
The shelter warms, a soft embrace.

So come, beloved, find your rest,
In the heart's stillness, we are blessed.
For in this place of light and song,
Together here is where we belong.

In the Shadow of His Wings

In quiet refuge, I find my peace,
His wings enfold, my fears now cease.
A gentle whisper, a guiding light,
In His embrace, I find my might.

The storms may rage, the world may flee,
Yet in His shadow, I'm truly free.
With every heartbeat, His love I know,
A sacred path, where faith will grow.

Beneath the heavens, I lift my prayer,
With gratitude woven in every tear.
For in the silence, His presence gleams,
A cherished promise, beyond my dreams.

In trials faced and burdens shared,
His strength upholds, my heart is bared.
In the shadow, I find my song,
Forever held, where I belong.

As days unfold, in grace I tread,
In every step, His love is spread.
In the shadow of His tender care,
I walk unafraid, my soul laid bare.

Cherished Stillness

In cherished stillness, I hear His call,
A whisper of grace, encompassing all.
The world fades away, burdens release,
In moments of quiet, I find my peace.

As dawn breaks softly, the light takes form,
His presence surrounds, a shelter warm.
In every heartbeat, His love intertwines,
In cherished stillness, the heart defines.

I close my eyes, to the chaos I yield,
In the sacred space, my wounds are healed.
Each breath a prayer, a promise so true,
In cherished stillness, I am made new.

With hands uplifted, I surrender all,
In every moment, I hear His call.
In the depth of silence, His truth ignites,
A cherished stillness, my soul delights.

As night descends, I find my rest,
In His warm embrace, my heart is blessed.
In cherished stillness, I walk the way,
With faith as my guide, each sacred day.

The Pause of Repentance

In the pause of repentance, my heart lays bare,
Reflecting on choices, the burdens I bear.
With humble spirit, I seek His grace,
In the stillness, I find my place.

Each misstep taken, a lesson learned,
For love's gentle call, my heart has yearned.
In the pause of repentance, I turn from the night,
Towards the dawn, where hope shines bright.

Seek forgiveness, the soul's true balm,
In His endless mercy, I find my calm.
With every tear, I release the past,
In the pause of repentance, my soul holds fast.

With faith rekindled, my spirit soars high,
In the embrace of the Divine, I die.
A resurrection awaits, purity's call,
In the pause of repentance, I rise from the fall.

So here I stand, renewed in my plight,
In the pause of repentance, I step into light.
With courage anew, I walk the path just,
In the grace of His hands, I place my trust.

A Retreat into Faith

In a retreat into faith, I lay my load,
With trust in Him, I walk the road.
Each step a journey, each breath a prayer,
In His gentle arms, I find my care.

The world may tremble, the skies may weep,
In this retreat, my spirit leaps.
Where shadows linger, His light breaks through,
In a retreat into faith, I am made new.

With every sunrise, my heart will sing,
In the joy of surrender, my soul takes wing.
Quietly beckoned, I rise to the call,
In a retreat into faith, I stand tall.

As mountains crumble and valleys dip low,
My heart anchored deep, in the love I know.
In His holy silence, I find my strength,
In a retreat into faith, I find my length.

With each falling leaf, I learn to let go,
In the stillness of trust, my spirit will grow.
In a retreat into faith, I set my face,
Towards brighter horizons, embraced by grace.

Refuge in Reverence

In silence we gather, hearts pure and bright,
Seeking the comfort in spiritual light.
Faith whispers softly, a warm, gentle breeze,
In the stillness, our souls find their ease.

Wings of the spirit, we rise from the dust,
In the bond of a prayer, we place all our trust.
With eyes turned to heaven, we feel the embrace,
In the refuge of reverence, we find our grace.

Sacred the moment, where souls intertwine,
A tapestry woven in love so divine.
Hearts join in chorus, a song of the free,
In the stillness of worship, we are meant to be.

Through trials and shadows, we walk hand in hand,
Each step a reminder, together we stand.
With faith as our shield, we're never alone,
In the refuge of reverence, together we've grown.

So let us remember, in joy or in strife,
Connection through spirit, the essence of life.
In the depth of our being, we seek and we find,
In the refuge of reverence, our hearts are aligned.

Chronicles of the Heart

Within the stillness, our stories unfold,
Chronicles written in courage and bold.
Each heartbeat a testament, a whisper of grace,
In the journey of life, we find our place.

Like stars in the heavens, our paths intertwine,
Sharing the burdens, our spirits align.
Moments of kindness, like gems from above,
In the chronicles of heart, we witness the love.

The echoes of laughter, the salt of our tears,
Mark chapters of growth through countless years.
In faith we gather, in hope we believe,
In the chronicles of heart, all souls can achieve.

Through valleys of sorrow, through mountains of joy,
We honor the memories, the dreams we employ.
With each passing season, our spirits grow strong,
In the chronicles of heart, we know we belong.

With every prayer spoken, with every song sung,
We weave together the old and the young.
Our tale is eternal, divinely imparted,
In the chronicles of heart, we remain open-hearted.

The Celestial Haven

In the quiet of dusk, where shadows take flight,
Lies a sacred sanctuary, bathed in soft light.
The heavens above, a vast tapestry rare,
In the celestial haven, we breathe in the air.

Stars dance like blessings, sent down from the high,
Gifting hope to our hearts, like a lullaby.
With each shining moment, we gather around,
In the celestial haven, true solace is found.

The whispers of angels, they guide us with care,
Illuminating paths, leading us there.
Through trials we wander, yet never alone,
In the celestial haven, we have all grown.

With hearts wide open, we share in the grace,
Finding unity's beauty in each warm embrace.
In the vastness of love, our spirits ascend,
In the celestial haven, our souls will mend.

Let us cherish these moments, like stars in the night,
For within this haven, our hearts soar in flight.
In togetherness anchored, through joy and through pain,
In the celestial haven, we shall forever remain.

Time on Holy Ground

Each second a blessing, a sacred decree,
On holy ground we stand, united and free.
In the echo of silence, our spirits arise,
With grace intertwined, like the vast, open skies.

Moments like whispers, they carry our prayers,
In the presence of the Divine, love's essence declares.
With each gentle step, we walk hand in hand,
On time's holy ground, where faith takes its stand.

In the warmth of the sun, in the chill of the night,
We gather as one, embraced by the light.
Through trials and triumphs, our hearts shall resound,
In the rhythm of time on this hallowed ground.

The sacred is woven in each breath that we take,
In the tapestry of life, with each choice we make.
Amidst joys and sorrows, we find the profound,
In the moments of stillness, on holy ground.

So let us remember, as time swiftly flows,
Each heartbeat a promise, each moment bestows.
In unity's embrace, may our hearts always pound,
In the journey of love, on this sacred ground.

Beneath the Canopy of Hope

Beneath the canopy, a shelter divine,
Where dreams of the faithful in whispers align.
Sunbeams like blessings, they dance and they play,
Guiding our spirits, come what may.

Each leaf a promise, each branch a prayer,
In the heart of the woods, our burdens laid bare.
Quiet reflections in a sacred embrace,
We find our way back to love's warm grace.

The winds carry whispers from far above,
Reminding us always we're cradled in love.
In shadows of giants, we gather our fears,
And let them be washed by the flow of our tears.

For hope is the light that will never depart,
Illuminating paths deep within every heart.
Beneath this canopy, we're never alone,
In unity's strength, we find our true home.

So let us rejoice in this holy design,
Together in silence, our spirits entwined.
With faith as our compass, we'll wander and roam,
Beneath the canopy, forever we'll bloom.

Balancing on Holy Ground

On holy ground where our feet gently tread,
We gather in reverence, the words gently said.
Each step is a prayer, each moment a song,
In the stillness we find where our souls truly belong.

With hearts open wide, we lift up our hands,
In whispers of gratitude, our spirit expands.
The sacred surrounds us, a veil drawn so near,
A balance of wonders, a dance free from fear.

As dawn breaks the darkness, we witness the light,
Each ray a reminder of grace in our sight.
We walk through the valleys, through shadows and glow,
Balancing on holy ground, we'll grow.

In moments of silence, in echoes of grace,
We're filled with the spirit that time can't erase.
Embracing the beauty that life has to share,
On this holy ground, we breathe in the air.

Together we stand as the sun sets and gleams,
Finding hope in our souls, igniting our dreams.
On holy ground, as the night softly falls,
We find strength in each other, where love gently calls.

The Embrace of Eternity

In the embrace of eternity, we find our peace,
A timeless connection where worries all cease.
Each moment a treasure, each heartbeat a glow,
In love's endless cycle, we're destined to flow.

The whispers of ages, they cradle us near,
With echoes of wisdom that soothe every fear.
As stars weave their stories across the night sky,
We touch the divine, through each tear that we cry.

For life is a journey, a wondrous array,
In the embrace of eternity, we choose to stay.
With faith as our anchor, we drift on the sea,
In depths of devotion, we're wholly set free.

Through laughter and sorrow, we gather our strength,
In love's gentle arms, we find infinite length.
A tapestry woven with each thread of grace,
In the embrace of eternity, we find our place.

So let us remember, as seasons unfold,
In the tapestry of life, we are woven in gold.
With hearts intertwined in a dance ever true,
In the embrace of eternity, love will renew.

Depths of Devotion

In the depths of devotion, we delve and explore,
In waters of spirit, our hearts start to soar.
With faith as our anchor, we plunge ever deep,
In silence we listen, in stillness we weep.

Through trials and triumphs, our spirits emerge,
Each moment a lesson, each wave a surge.
With prayers as our lifeline, we navigate wide,
In the depths of devotion, our souls will abide.

The whispers of ages reflect in our eyes,
In the realms of the sacred, our true nature lies.
With hearts full of yearning, we seek and we find,
In the depths of devotion, our spirits unwind.

For love is a river that endlessly flows,
In the depths of our journeys, true wisdom it shows.
As we dive ever deeper, we're changed by the grace,
In the depths of devotion, we find our safe space.

So let us embrace, in this ocean we tread,
With hearts intertwined, in communion we're led.
In the depths of devotion, our souls intertwine,
Together in faith, forever we shine.

Under the Cloak of Trust

In shadows cast by faith's embrace,
We find the light, a sacred place.
With every step, our hearts align,
In trust we walk, in love, divine.

Through trials faced, the spirit grows,
In whispers soft, the spirit glows.
Under the cloak, we stand as one,
In harmony 'til the race is run.

Embraced by grace, we seek to know,
The pathways where the faithful go.
Bound by a trust that never fails,
We soar above life's darkest trails.

With gratitude, our voices rise,
In prayers that reach the endless skies.
For in this bond, our souls find rest,
In every heart, His love confessed.

So let us walk, hand in hand,

Through valleys deep, across the land.
In unity, we carry the light,
Under the cloak, our spirits bright.

Pilgrimage of the Undisturbed

With footsteps light on ancient ground,
We seek the peace that can be found.
Upon this path, our hearts take flight,
In silence sharp, we find the light.

In sacred groves where stillness reigns,
Each moment pure, the spirit gains.
A pilgrimage for souls refined,
In still waters, true love aligned.

The journey's long, yet we embrace,
The gentle touch of endless grace.
With every breath, a prayer ascends,
In quietude, the heart transcends.

Through trials faced, we're undeterred,
In solemn paths, our faith assured.
The world may roar, yet here we stand,
In the embrace of the divine hand.

Oh, pilgrim soul, do not despair,
For peace awaits, as you prepare.
In every step, let love abide,
In pilgrimage, the spirit's guide.

Harbors of the Spirit

In tranquil shores, the spirit rests,
Among the hills where silence nests.
A refuge found, where none can sway,
In harbors safe, we long to stay.

With tides that ebb and flow like grace,
We find our strength in this embrace.
The whispers of the winds remind,
Of love eternal, pure and kind.

In sheltered nooks where hearts unite,
We gather strength in soft twilight.
The stars above, a guiding song,
In harbors true, we all belong.

Through storms we sail, yet fear not, stay,
For faith will guide our every way.
As spirit's harbor, we are one,
Together rise, until we've won.

In these sweet shores, our hopes take flight,
Embraced by love's consuming light.
In timeless grace, our souls secure,
In harbors bold, we shall endure.

Still Waters of Belief

By still waters flows a stream of prayer,
In quietude, we sense the care.
With gentle ripples, hearts awake,
In faith's embrace, we choose to take.

The murmur of the leaves above,
In perfect peace, we feel His love.
A sanctuary, soft and clear,
In still waters, we have no fear.

Each moment steals the weight of doubt,
In solitude, our souls we scout.
Beneath the sky, where dreams unfold,
In stillness found, we gather gold.

With open hearts, we seek to find,
The sacred truths that are entwined.
In waters deep, we dip our hands,
And grasp the grace, as His love expands.

We drink of hope, of joy, of peace,
In faith's embrace, our burdens cease.
With every breath, a promise made,
In still waters, our fears shall fade.

A Prayerful Respite

In quiet corners, hearts unite,
We seek the calm, away from night.
With whispered hopes, our spirits soar,
In prayerful breath, we find the door.

Each moment held, a sacred trust,
In faith we gather, wise and just.
With every sigh, release the weight,
In stillness found, our souls await.

The light within, a gentle guide,
In solitude, we bide our tide.
With fervent hearts, we reach above,
Embraced by grace, we feel the love.

Through trials faced, in earnest plea,
We find our strength, through unity.
In prayerful respite, peace we trace,
The hands of heaven, our saving grace.

The Holy Hour

In the hush of twilight's glow,
We gather here, our spirits flow.
Within this hour, all doubts depart,
In sacred time, we tune our heart.

The candles flicker, shadows dance,
Each moment calls, a holy chance.
To lift our eyes, in wonder stare,
To feel the weight of love and care.

With hands uplifted, praises rise,
Our voices merge, beneath the skies.
In silent prayer, we seek the light,
The holy hour, a gift of night.

Beneath the stars, our hopes align,
In this embrace, divinity's sign.
We dwell in peace, our burdens shed,
In grateful hearts, the spirit led.

In the Embrace of Mercy

When shadows fall and fears abound,
We turn to You, our hope is found.
In mercy's arms, we take our rest,
Embraced by love, forever blessed.

Each tear we shed, a sacred plea,
In grace, we find our liberty.
The broken heart, restored anew,
In mercy's light, we live and brew.

With every prayer, a longing grows,
To grasp the peace that always flows.
In gentle whispers, You remind,
In mercy's love, we seek and find.

Through paths of trials, we walk with faith,
In mercy's hands, we find our place.
Together united, we face the dawn,
In Your embrace, we are reborn.

The Still Waters of Grace

In still waters, our souls find peace,
Where worries fade, and troubles cease.
With every breath, we drink of light,
In grace, we soar, beyond our sight.

The gentle ripples, a soothing song,
With every note, we know we belong.
In nature's calm, the heart does mend,
In quietude, our spirits blend.

The world outside, a distant sound,
In stillness found, our truth is crowned.
With faith as anchor, we shall tread,
To crystal springs, where hope is fed.

With open arms, we seek the way,
In grace's light, we choose to stay.
In still waters, life flows anew,
In every moment, we are true.

Sheltered Beneath Grace

In whispers soft, the heavens call,
Where mercy rains, we rise and fall.
A gentle hand upon our plight,
In shadows deep, we find the light.

With faith as strong as ancient trees,
We bend but do not break with ease.
The warmth of love, a sacred place,
Forever held, we're housed in grace.

Through trials fierce, our spirits soar,
For every wound, we seek the more.
In unity, our hearts embrace,
Together in this boundless space.

Though storms may rage and doubts may sway,
We trust the path, we kneel and pray.
For in this space where mercy flows,
A deeper truth within us grows.

So let us walk, hand in hand,
Through valleys low, on sacred land.
With hearts aflame and spirits free,
We'll dwell where love and grace decree.

The Garden of Quietude

In corners still, the lilies sigh,
Where silence speaks and soft winds fly.
Each petal glows with sacred hue,
In peace we find the hope anew.

The whispering trees with arms outstretched,
In every leaf, a promise etched.
With every step on hallowed ground,
In nature's heart, grace can be found.

The brook that sings a tender song,
Reminds us where our hearts belong.
With every sound, the earth will tell,
Of love that binds us, all is well.

Beneath the stars, the night unfolds,
Our stories etched in cosmic gold.
In moments still, our spirits bloom,
In quietude, dispelling gloom.

So linger here, no need to rush,
In sacred stillness find the hush.
With open hearts, embrace the night,
In every shadow, seek the light.

Moments Unseen

In fleeting time, the world unfolds,
Each breath a gift, a tale retold.
The gentle touch of unseen grace,
In whispered prayers, we find our place.

In laughter shared and sorrows borne,
The threads of love are never torn.
For every glance, a story weaves,
In hidden ways, the spirit leaves.

With hearts attuned to every sigh,
We find the sacred in the sky.
In every dawn that greets the day,
The moments lost are here to stay.

Through trials faced and joy embraced,
In silence filled, our fears erased.
For every touch and smile unseen,
The love remains, forever keen.

So cherish now, each heartbeat's chime,
In this vast dance of space and time.
With humble hearts, we seek to glean,
The beauty found in moments unseen.

The Light in the Stillness

In quiet dawn, the world awakes,
With gentle grace, our spirit shakes.
Each ray of sun, a promise near,
In stillness found, we calm our fear.

The whispers of the morning breeze,
Bring hope anew as hearts find ease.
In every shadow, light will play,
Guiding the lost along the way.

With every pause, divine we seek,
In moments soft, the spirit speaks.
The heart attunes to nature's song,
In stillness, we learn to belong.

Through trials faced and dreams held close,
The light within, we need the most.
In every tear, a lesson learned,
In every heart, a fire burned.

So let us find in silence deep,
The treasures there, our souls will keep.
For in the still, the love shines bright,
A beacon clear, our guiding light.

The Spiritual Shelter

In the quiet embrace of the dawn,
Faith wraps around like a gentle shawl.
Whispers of hope echo softly within,
In the stillness, we feel the call.

Hands raised high, we seek the light,
Guided by love that heals the strife.
Here in this haven, hearts take flight,
United in faith, we find our life.

Beneath the vastness of heaven's grace,
Every prayer rises, a sacred plea.
In this shelter, we find our place,
Where souls are free, eternally.

As the sun sets, shadows retreat,
In the warmth of love, fears dissolve.
With open hearts, we share the feast,
In the spirit's bond, we are whole.

Together we walk on this blessed path,
With faith as our shield, and hope our guide.
In the shelter of grace, we find our wrath,
Transformed to love, forever tied.

Interlude of the Faithful

In moments serene, we pause to reflect,
The voice of the heavens calls us to peace.
With each gentle breath, we seek to connect,
In the stillness, our worries cease.

Gathered as one in sacred space,
The chorus of hearts sings a tune.
With hands intertwined, we seek solace,
Together beneath the same moon.

The laughter of children, a heavenly sound,
Echoing joy in the air we share.
In the interlude, love knows no bounds,
A testament of faith everywhere.

As the day wanes, we light our way,
With candles aglow, hope shines bright.
In this shared moment, we come to pray,
Finding strength in each warm light.

With spirits uplifted, we rise anew,
In the truth of our bonds, divine grace flows.
In this interlude, our love rings true,
For in faith, the beauty of life grows.

Resting in Righteousness

In the garden of grace, we lay our heads,
Where the petals whisper wisdom untold.
Resting in righteousness, our hearts are fed,
In the arms of love, we find our gold.

Through trials faced, we find our way,
With faith as our compass, we journey on.
In the quiet moments, we pause to pray,
In the embrace of night, we are drawn.

Under the stars, our worries cease,
In every heartbeat, we find our peace.
With every dawn, new mercies arise,
In the light of love, our spirits rise.

In the stillness of night, we close our eyes,
Finding solace in the sacred trust.
With open hearts, we reach for the skies,
In righteousness, we find what is just.

Together we stand, strong and free,
In the light of truth, we gather near.
Resting in righteousness, we shall see,
The promise of love, forever clear.

Sacred Silence of the Soul

In the sacred silence where shadows dwell,
The soul whispers truths, soft as the night.
In this quiet realm, we share a spell,
Touching the divine, in the still light.

With hearts attuned to the unseen grace,
Each moment unfolds in gentle flow.
In sacred silence, we find our place,
As love's gentle hand begins to sow.

In the absence of noise, clarity reigns,
The echo of faith lingers in the air.
In this sacred hush, a balm for pains,
Where hope flowers softly, free from care.

With eyes closed tight, we journey deep,
Through valleys of peace, we roam as one.
In the silence, promises we keep,
Guided by light, till the day is done.

As night embraces, we find our peace,
In the sacred silence, we learn to believe.
With hearts laid bare, we release,
In this holy stillness, we shall receive.

A Pilgrim's Pause

In quiet paths where footsteps tread,
I find the whispers of the dead.
Each stone, a tale, each tree, a sign,
In sacred stillness, I align.

The morning dew on grass does gleam,
A fleeting glimpse, a holy dream.
With every breath, I seek the light,
In shadows deep, I find my sight.

The clouds above, they shift and sway,
Divine reminders of the day.
In nature's arms, I find my way,
A pilgrim's heart, forever stay.

With each soft prayer, my spirit soars,
I open wide the ancient doors.
In solitude, my soul's embrace,
I feel the warmth of His grace.

At journey's end, I stand in peace,
Released from doubt, my fears cease.
A pilgrim's pause, I breathe and see,
In sacred love, I am set free.

Beneath the Veil of Time

In shadows deep, where secrets lie,
Beneath the veil, I search the sky.
The echoes of the ages past,
In silent whispers, shadows cast.

Each moment counts, each heartbeat sings,
The fleeting grace that stillness brings.
With every breath, I glimpse the divine,
In timeless dance, my soul entwined.

Through seasons' change, the cycle flows,
In winter's chill, in summer's glow.
The sacred pulse of life unfolds,
In every story, truth retold.

Beneath the stars, a witness stands,
The universe, in gentle hands.
Awakened dreams, in night's embrace,
I seek the light, I find His face.

In stillness found, my heart takes wing,
Embracing all the joy that springs.
Beneath the veil, a path I find,
With faith as guide, my soul aligned.

Sanctuary of Stillness

In the quiet grove where shadows dwell,
I hear the sacred stories tell.
The gentle rustle of the leaves,
A melody that softly weaves.

Within this space, my spirit sighs,
In tranquil grace, my worries die.
As sunlight filters through the trees,
I feel the comfort of His peace.

The brook's sweet song flows clear and true,
A liquid prayer that flows anew.
With every drop, a promise made,
In sanctuary, fears do fade.

The flowers bloom, a vibrant hue,
In nature's arms, my heart breaks through.
Each petal soft, each fragrance bright,
In stillness found, I taste the light.

Here in this haven, love abounds,
In sacred stillness, joy resounds.
A sanctuary, firm and long,
In silence, I discover song.

Embracing the Eternal

In the embrace of endless skies,
I seek the truth where wisdom lies.
Each moment fleeting, yet divine,
In love's embrace, my heart aligns.

Eternal grace flows like a stream,
Through valleys low, in mountains' gleam.
Each heartbeat whispers ancient tales,
Of love's sweet journey, never fails.

Within the stillness, I can hear,
The distant call, the sacred near.
With open arms, I welcome light,
In shadows cast, I find my sight.

Embracing all that life can bring,
In every joy, in every sting.
The tapestry of time unfolds,
In His embrace, my soul consoled.

With every dawn, I rise anew,
In every dusk, I hold the view.
Embracing all, I find my way,
In love that shines, night turns to day.

Communion of the Heart

In silent prayer, our souls entwine,
With whispers soft, divinity divine.
A holy bond, in love's embrace,
We gather here, seek sacred space.

Where faith ignites the flame we share,
In every breath, we find His care.
A unity, both pure and blessed,
In harmony, we find our rest.

Through trials faced, we hold our ground,
In troubled times, His grace is found.
He guides us on through darkest night,
With love's own hand, we grasp His light.

With hearts aligned and spirits free,
We walk as one, in unity.
Each step we take, in presence strong,
In every heart, a sacred song.

So let us rise, in faith we stand,
United now, we hold His hand.
In communion sweet, our hearts will heal,
In every prayer, His love we feel.

The Oasis of Grace

In deserts dry, where shadows creep,
Your mercy flows, our souls to keep.
A gentle stream, so pure and bright,
In every heart, You are our light.

In quietude, we find our peace,
Your love, a well, that will not cease.
With every drop, our thirst is quenched,
In You, dear Lord, our hopes are drenched.

The sun may scorch, the world may fade,
Yet in Your arms, our fears are laid.
A sanctuary from the storm,
In grace, we find our spirits warm.

With grateful hearts and lifted eyes,
We dance and sing, we shall arise.
In every moment, pain does cease,
Within Your grace, we find our peace.

Together here, we walk anew,
In love's embrace, the path is true.
An oasis vast, where spirits soar,
In joy and light, we're ever more.

Where Light Abides

In shadows deep, Your love remains,
A beacon bright that breaks our chains.
Your guiding hand, it shows the way,
In every heart, Your hope will stay.

Where darkness looms, we seek Your face,
In every trial, we find Your grace.
With hearts alight, we learn to fight,
In trust and faith, we find our light.

Your gentle whispers soothe our doubt,
In silence strong, You call us out.
To walk beside, to serve and lead,
In every thought, Your love we seed.

As stars align in velvet skies,
With every breath, our spirits rise.
For in Your name, our fears subside,
In every heart, where Light abides.

With arms outstretched, we seek to share,
A world of love, a world of prayer.
In unity, we join the tide,
Where souls awaken, and hope is wide.

The Cloistered Spirit

Within the walls of sacred grace,
We find a stillness, a holy space.
With prayers like petals, soft they fall,
In silence deep, we hear Your call.

Our thoughts in chant, our hearts in sync,
In every sigh, we cease to think.
A cloistered soul, in love confined,
With faith so bold, we seek to find.

In morning light and evening's glow,
We offer thanks for all we know.
A gentle breeze, a whispered plea,
In every moment, we are free.

Through trials faced and burdens borne,
In fellowship, we are reborn.
With every step, our spirits climb,
In every prayer, we seek Your rhyme.

So let us dwell, in peace abide,
With hearts of joy, and arms open wide.
In cloistered love, we find our way,
Together here, we humbly stay.